We don't stop playing because we grow old; we grow old because we stop playing.

Seriously I'm 50?
My Drink & Advice Book

50 Drink
Recipes

from my friends
And 50 other things I need to remember
now
that I'm 50!

∞

For Darren T

Books With Soul
Somewhere in the desert, sea and forest.
www.bookswithsoul.com
∞
Books with Soul supports copyright for all authors.
Thank you for purchasing a copyrighted edition of this book.
First Edition 2018

ISBN 13- 978-1-949325-29-4

This book, "Seriously, I'm 50"—
belongs to a new
50- year old as named below.
Welcome to the 50 club. Remember, the numbers
only get
higher from here.

_____

Date: _____

Given by: _____

Seriously?

So, you're 50! Fantastic! Fifty will be the youngest you will ever be in your life-- from here on out.

Fifty, fifty, fifty, fifty, fifty, fifty. Roll it around on your tongue and get used to it. Fifty. Yes, You're in the 50 club now and that changes everything.

Everything.

Soon you will start forgetting things, experience a few more ache and pains, and lose a little hair.

Fifty. Yes, it sounds like a big word. Fifty

Don't fret, this book will help ease the pain.

Inside this book, write things you don't want to forget. Write down your friends' favorite shots or drinks and keep this notebook near your bar. Or better yet, ask them to write their favorite drink or shot next time they come over and create your own bar book.

There's also 50 pages for pieces of advice, toasts or quotes you might want to remember before you forget, and 50 pages to write whatever you want to remember.

Enjoy the five zero year. Hopefully with pen in hand, YOU will remember the best of it.

Happy 50th

Birthday!

"You can't go back and change the beginning, but you can start where you are and change the ending."

-unknown

Seriously I'm 50?
My drink & advice book.

Table of contents:

Section I:
50 One-page Recipes
shot/shooter/drink or favorite wine
(from my friends)

Section II:
50 Pieces of Advice, Toasts, Quotes
from friends & family

Section III:
50 Important Things to Remember
Now that I'm 50! Write them down
in this section, before you forget.

Complete this book over the next year or until you're facing the 60's.
Ask your friends to write down their favorite shot or drink and a piece of advice.
Keep it next to your favorite drinking spot.
Someday, you'll look back and be shocked... because you'll forget you ever did this... (Yes, that's what happens with age).

It does not matter how slowly you go, just so you don't stop -Confucius

Section I:

50 drink recipes from my friends
(shot/shooter/drink or wine)

_____

Here's a toast to you on your 50th birthday! Try making a drink a friend loves.

Name of Person & shot/shooter/drink/wine

_____

If you want to fly give up everything that weighs you down.

Name of Person &
shot/shooter/drink/wine

Name of Person &
shot/shooter/drink/wine

_____

Name of Person &
shot/shooter/drink/wine

_____

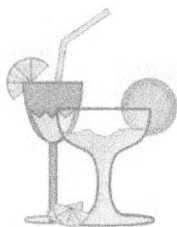

Don't stop seeing the world from a child-like perspective.

Name of Person &
shot/shooter/drink/wine

_____

Name of Person &
shot/shooter/drink/wine

Name of Person &
shot/shooter/drink/wine

_____

Live, Laugh, Love
Why not? Do you
know of a better
way to live?

Name of Person & shot/shooter/drink/wine

Name of Person & shot/shooter/drink/wine

_____

Name of Person &
shot/shooter/drink/wine

Live for the day, like it is your last.

Name of Person &
shot/shooter/drink/wine

_____

Name of Person &
shot/shooter/drink/wine

———————

Name of Person & shot/shooter/drink/wine

The best is yet to come.

Name of Person &
shot/shooter/drink/wine

———————

Name of Person & shot/shooter/drink/wine

_____

Name of Person &
shot/shooter/drink/wine

———————

On a certain occasion beer could be considered a breakfast food.

Name of Person &
shot/shooter/drink/wine

_____

Name of Person &
shot/shooter/drink/wine

Name of Person &
shot/shooter/drink/wine

———————

"Wrinkles should merely indicate where the smiles have been."
— **Mark Twain**

I hope you wrinkle.

Name of Person & shot/shooter/drink/wine

Name of Person &
shot/shooter/drink/wine

_____

Name of Person &
shot/shooter/drink/wine

Don't worry, Be happy!

Name of Person &
shot/shooter/drink/wine

Name of Person &
shot/shooter/drink/wine

––––––––––

Name of Person & shot/shooter/drink/wine

A smile is a crooked line that sets things straight.
- Phyllis Diller

Name of Person &
shot/shooter/drink/wine

_____

Name of Person & shot/shooter/drink/wine

_____

Name of Person &
shot/shooter/drink/wine

_____

The life I live is
created by the
story I tell.
-Abraham Hicks

Name of Person &
shot/shooter/drink/wine

_____

Name of Person &
shot/shooter/drink/wine

_____

Name of Person &
shot/shooter/drink/wine

_____

It is only with the heart that one can see rightly; what is essential is invisible to the eye.
-Antoine De Saint-Exupery

Name of Person &
shot/shooter/drink/wine

Name of Person &
shot/shooter/drink/wine

_____

Name of Person &
shot/shooter/drink/wine

———————

Never give up.

Name of Person &
shot/shooter/drink/wine

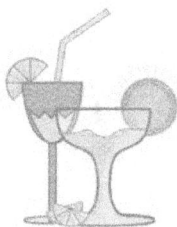

Name of Person &
shot/shooter/drink/wine

_____

Name of Person &
shot/shooter/drink/wine

Find your happy place.

Name of Person &
shot/shooter/drink/wine

———————

Name of Person & shot/shooter/drink/wine

_____

Name of Person & shot/shooter/drink/wine

_____

The report of my death was an exaggeration.
Mark Twain

Name of Person & shot/shooter/drink/wine

_____

Name of Person &
shot/shooter/drink/wine

————————

Name of Person &
shot/shooter/drink/wine

_____

Nothing is permanent in this wicked world, not even our troubles.
-Charlie Chaplin

Name of Person &
shot/shooter/drink/wine

_____

Name of Person &
shot/shooter/drink/wine

_____

Name of Person & shot/shooter/drink/wine

_____

Live in the moment.

Name of Person &
shot/shooter/drink/wine

Name of Person &
shot/shooter/drink/wine

_____

Name of Person &
shot/shooter/drink/wine

_____

Name of Person &
shot/shooter/drink/wine

_____

Section II:

50 pieces of Advice for your 50th Year

Trust your crazy ideas.

Advice from

_____

Advice from

_____

Life is a balance of
holding on and
letting go.
-Rumi

Advice from

_____

Advice from

_____

"The man who does not read has no advantage over the man who cannot read."
— **Mark Twain**

Advice from

_____

Advice from

_____

Advice from

_____

You've always had the power my dear, you just had to learn it for yourself.
-The Wizard of Oz

Advice from

_____

Advice from

_____

Advice from

_____

Do one (secret) good thing today and tell no one.

Advice from

_____

Advice from

_____

Advice from

_____

The best view comes after the hardest climb.

Advice from

_____

Advice from

_____

Advice from

_____

Believe in yourself.

Advice from

_____

Advice from

_____

Advice from

_____

Human beings are amazing. If they set their mind, plan and never give up, they can accomplish anything.

Advice from

_____

Advice from

_____

Advice from

_____

Follow your dreams they know the way.

Advice from

_____

Advice from

_____

Advice from

_____

Enjoy the little things in life, because someday you will look back and realize they were the big things.

Advice from

_____

Advice from

_____

Advice from

_____

It's free to be kind.

Advice from

_____

Advice from

_____

Advice from

_____

one small positive thought in the morning can change your day.
-*Dalia Lama*

Advice from

_____

Advice from

_____

Advice from

_____

Only a boring person is bored.

Advice from

_____

Advice from

_____

Advice from

_____

Advice from

_____

Life can be a
fairytale, write
your happy
ending.

Advice from

_____

Advice from

_____

Advice from

_____

"What would men be without women? Scarce, sir...mighty scarce."
— **Mark Twain**

Advice from

_____

Advice from

_____

Advice from

_____

Don't save the best for last.

Advice from

_____

Advice from

_____

Advice from

_____

Take the road less
traveled and open
your eyes.

Advice from

_____

Advice from

_____

Advice from

_____

Section III:

50 things I need to remember
(before I forget)

Will it be easy? Nope. Will it be worth it? Absolutely.

I need to remember this:

_____

I need to remember this:

_____

I need to remember this:

_____

I need to remember this:

———————

Believe you can &
you're halfway
there.
    -T. Roosevelt

I need to remember this:

_____

I need to remember this:

_____

I need to remember this:

_____

I need to remember this:

_____

Take the risk or lose the chance.

I need to remember this:

_____

I need to remember this:

_____

I need to remember this:

_____

I need to remember this:

———————

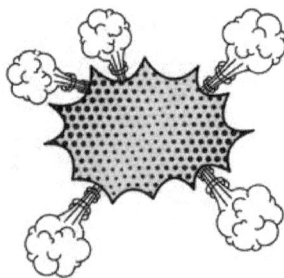

The trouble is, you think you have time.

I need to remember this:

I need to remember this:

_____

I need to remember this:

_____

I need to remember this:

_____

Storms don't last forever.

I need to remember this:

_____

I need to remember this:

_____

I need to remember this:

_____

I need to remember this:

_____

There are so many beautiful reasons to be happy.

I need to remember this:

_____

I need to remember this:

_____

I need to remember this:

_____

I need to remember this:

_____

Stay humble, work hard and be kind.

I need to remember this:

_____

I need to remember this:

_____

I need to remember this:

_____

I need to remember this:

_____

Enjoy the journey.

I need to remember this:

_____

I need to remember this:

_____

I need to remember this:

———————————

I need to remember this:

_____

Every saint has a past and every sinner a future.
-Oscar Wilde

I need to remember this:

_____

I need to remember this:

_____

I need to remember this:

_____

I need to remember this:

_____

I have not failed
I've just found
10,000 ways that
won't work.
-Thomas Edison

I need to remember this:

———————

I need to remember this:

_____

I need to remember this:

_____

I need to remember this:

_____

When life gets blurry adjust your focus.

I need to remember this:

_____

I need to remember this:

_____

I need to remember this:

———————

I need to remember this:

Don't count the days. Make the days count.

I need to remember this:

_____

I need to remember this:

_____

I need to remember this:

_____

I need to remember this:

———————

It's free to be kind.

I need to remember this:

_____

I need to remember this:

_____

Other Books With Soul:
Words I want to Say
Every Breath- A Journal of Gratitude & Blessings
Crazy Ramblings of a Pregnant Woman
Remember When: Guest Book
Camp Memories
Reflections from the Beach
The Plan
The Adventures of US
Reflections of My Year
Pregnancy Journal: When We Were One
My little book I write shit down in
Wish: A book of wishes

Anniversary editions available on Amazon:
1st Anniversary: One Epic Year
5th Anniversary: Five Epic Years
10th Anniversary: Ten Epic Years
15th Anniversary: Fifteen Epic Years
20th Anniversary: Twenty Epic Years
25th Anniversary: Twenty-five Epic Years
30th Anniversary: Thirty Epic Years
35th Anniversary: Thirty-five Epic Years
40th Anniversary: Forty Epic Years
45th Anniversary: Forty-five Epic Years
50th Anniversary: Fifty Epic Years

Perfect Anniversary Gift

Books With Soul

Books with Soul believes in sharing gifts that inspire and motivate others to create memories and keep a record of the story of their life.

What if... you had a record of your memories or someone you loved?

INSPIRATION COMES IN ALL SIZES, SHAPES & IDEAS

WE believe every life is worth a few written words to pass on or reflect on in the future. You don't have to be an author to tell the story of your life. Just be you. Today will someday be the good old days, remember them.

Books with Soul offers inspirational journals with questions & thoughts to help record memories for the most novice of journalers. Birthday, milestones, wedding and baby gifts. Help someone write their life story.

Questions? Email info@bookswithsoul.com

We appreciate every reader, every traveler and recorder of history. We would love if you took the time to write a review on Amazon and let us know if the books motivated you.

Find more journals, inspiration, diaries, coloring books and gifts for every milestone at:

www.bookswithsoul.com

If you would like to have a personalized journal for an organization, company, group, club, or activity, contact Books with Soul. Special unique journals in 25 quantities or more can be created.

*if someone bought you this journal, pay it forward and buy a journal
for someone you care about.
Help them become more positive in life, love and family.

Thank you!
If this make you even a little bit more positive, **please leave a review on Amazon!** Let's help the world become more positive. Imagine if everyone did this every morning!

Sign up for our newsletter on sales and giveaways from Bookswithsoul.com

Books with Soul ™

was inspired from a lover of music and life, who believed in the soul. He had a collection of wonderful things. Physical memories you could read, touch, and listen to- including thousands of vinyl albums.

Old school music, that lasts forever. In 2018, he passed away from brain cancer, but his memory lives on as others go old school. Collect pieces of your history, put pencil to paper, and record written memories.

A physical book will not be lost in the cloud and will last longer than a lifetime.

Keep a record of the story of your life. Your Words. Your Pages.

This is for you Mark.

Bookswithsoul.com
Your Words. Your Pages.

Thanks for taking the time to collect a book you will have around for a lifetime.

Keep this book somewhere safe.

Hide it, share it or leave it for someone you love.
START A YEARLY COLLECTION.

OR

GIFT ONE AS A SPECIAL GIFT

A VARIETY OF JOURNALS EXIST: TRY ONE

WITH DAILY INSPIRATIONAL QUOTES,

OR WRITING PROMPTS TO KEEP YOU

WRITING.

VISIT THE WEBSITE FOR SALES & SWAG

Bookswithsoul.com
Your Words. Your Pages.

Life is beautiful.